THE REVELATION

GOD'S HAND IN WORLD AFFAIRS

By Ronnie C. Antoine

Acknowledgements

3

My name is Ronnie C. Antoine, and I am the author of this book and of my first publication in December 2020 titled *The Prophet Speaks*. I want to give credit to my beautiful daughter Raina once again for the time, devotion, and attentiveness she applied in the preparation and publishing of this book. I am forever grateful.

Table Of Contents

From the book of Genesis to the book of Revelation, the Bible is filled with prophecies showing God and how he has intervened in world affairs. The creator of the universe does not make his plans for fanciful, impulsive, or temperamental reasons. His second coming will make the difference between life and death for the human race. Preachers who foolishly proclaim "Tonight is the night" are doing a grave disservice to their listeners. Jesus Christ prophesied that just before his return there will be "famines" (lack of food) and "pestilences" (disease epidemics). At this time we are seeing the beginning of these curses that will increase and in turn have a massive effect on our entire way of life!

Yet all of these problems are just the beginning of the story. Soon, the ultimate personification of the Antichrist will appear on the world scene. First, his presence will be that of a kind and gentle "peace-maker". Then he will gradually get more and more authority. His authority will be enhanced by false miracles that Satan will perform through him (Revelation 13:13). For Satan the Devil is glad to have you "believe in Christ" - as long as your Christ is a false one, provided that he can lead you to a church led by blinded, rejecting, theologians. As Jesus said: "If the blind leads the blind, both will fall into a ditch" (Matthew 15:14).

Satan is the "Great Deceiver", who actively continues to deceive the entire world. He was cast to the Earth, and his angels were cast out with him (Revelation 12:9). One-third of the angels joined Lucifer (Revelation 12:3, 4). Satan uses every conceivable approach to deceive and destroy people. His demons can appear and pose as righteous people, even clergymen. And Satan will appear as a glorious angel of light with the power to call fire down from Heaven. He will impersonate Jesus, but you have been forewarned, so don't fall for it. When Jesus comes, every eye will see him (Revelation 1:7). He will remain in the clouds and not even touch the earth (1 Thessalonians 4:17).

1

What Happened in Heaven as a Consequence of Lucifer's Rebellion?

"And war broke out in Heaven; Michael and his angels fought with the dragon; and the dragon and his angels fought, but they did not prevail, nor was a place found for them in heaven any longer. So the great dragon was cast out, that serpent of old, called the devil and satan, who deceives the whole world; he was cast to the earth, and his angels were cast out with him" (Revelation 12:7-9).

Most people in the world are being deceived by an evil genius bent on destroying their lives - a brilliant mastermind called the Devil, or Satan. But this dark prince is much more than what you might think... many say he's just a devious mythical figure, but the Bible says he's very real, and he's deceiving families, churches, and even nations to increase sorrow and pain. Satan wants people to worship him. He even tried to persuade Jesus to do so. Satan will try to force people to worship him or else be killed (Revelation 13:15).

That's why it is so important to resist Satan and all his traps and when we realize when he is trying to attack us, we must simply stop and pray this specific prayer:

"May God rebuke Satan and all his evil spirits who wander through the world for the ruin of souls. Amen."

Repent, or else I will come unto thee quickly, and I will fight against them with the sword of my mouth (Revelation 2:16). Notwithstanding I have a few things against thee, because thou sufferest that woman Jezebel, which called herself a prophetess, to teach and seduce my servants to commit fornication, and to eat things sacrificed with idols.

And I gave her the chance to repent her fornication; and she repented not (Revelation 2:20-21). Behold, I will cast her into a bed, and them that commit adultery with her into great tribulation, except they repent of their deeds. And I will kill her children with death; and all the churches shall know that I am he which searcheth the reins and hearts; and I will give unto every one of you according to your works (Revelation 2:22-23).

Now for one moment if Jezebel would have stopped and chose to take the offer of repenting her sins to God, neither her nor her children's lives would have been threatened.

2

To Be Able to Acknowledge When You're Committing Sinful Acts Requires Wisdom and Strength.

It is easy to put these sinful acts to a halt and to decide to come to God in prayer. When we repent he does not hesitate to forgive us and save our souls.

After the thousand years are over, Satan will be freed from his prison. He will seek to go out into the world deceiving entire nations. He will bring them all together in battle; he will seek out as many people to recruit as there are grains of sand on the seashore. They spread out over the earth and surrounded the camp made up of God's people.

However, fire was cast down from Heaven and destroyed them all. The Devil, who had deceived them, was thrown into the Lake of Fire and Sulfur, where the beast and the false prophet had already been thrown. They are to be tormented day and night for an eternity (Revelation 20:7-10).

3

Now Let Us Look at the Return of Jesus.

"These words are true and trustworthy," said the angel. Then the Lord God, who gives his spirit to the prophets has sent his angels to show his servants what will happen very soon. "Listen!" says Jesus. "I am coming soon! Happy are those who obey the prophetic words in this book!"

"I, John, have heard and seen all these things and when I finished hearing and seeing them, I fell down at the feet of the angel who had shown me these things, and I was about to worship God!" and he said to me, "Do not keep the prophetic words of this book a secret because the time is near when all this will happen. Whoever is evil must go on doing evil, whoever is filthy must go on being filthy. Whoever is good must go on doing good, and whoever is holy must go on being holy."

"Listen!" says Jesus. "I am coming soon! I will bring my rewards with me, to give to each one according to what he has done. I am the First and the Last, the Beginning and the End."

Happy are those who wash their robes clean and so have the right to eat the fruit from the tree of life and to go through the gates into the city. But outside the city are the perverts and those who practice magic, the immoral and the murderers, those who worship idols and those who are liars both in words and deeds.

"I, Jesus, have sent my angel to announce these things to you in the churches. I am descended from the Family of David; I am the bright and morning star. The spirit and the Bride say, come!" Come, whoever is thirsty; accept the water of life as a gift, whoever wants it (Revelation 22:6-17).

Man is not immortal, he is subject to die.

God's people will indeed have eternal life now.

Eternal life is a new and miraculous Jesus-filled life.

This life starts at conversion and will continue on in Heaven.

God's promise is that his faithful people, who now have eternal life, won't suffer the second death (Revelation 2:11), which has no resurrection. In the first death, we all must die. It does not stop eternal life, however. It continues in Heaven after the Resurrection.

4

I Saw a New Heaven and a New Earth.

The first Heaven and Earth disappeared, and the sea vanished. Then I see the Holy City, which is the New Jerusalem, coming out of Heaven from God, prepared and ready, as a bride to meet her husband. Then there was a loud voice that spoke from the throne.

"God's home is with the people! God will be with them, and he will be their God. He will wipe away all tears from their eyes. There will be no more death, grief, crying, or pain, for the former things have passed away" (Revelation 21:1-4). He who sat upon the throne said, "Behold, I make all things new", and said unto me, "For these words are true and faithful. It is done. I am the Alpha and Omega, the beginning and the end, I will give unto him that thirst of the Fountain of the Water of Life freely. He that overcometh shall inherit all things; I will be his God and he shall be my son" (Revelation 21:1-7).

The fearful, the unbelieving, the abominable, the murderers, the sorcerers, the whore mongers, the liars, and the idolaters will all have a place in the Lake that burns with fire and brimstone. This is the second death. Jesus was referred to as King of the East by those who assisted him in Heaven. In the prophecies Heaven is referred to as "the East", hence making Jesus the King of Heaven.

In Ezekiel 43:2, it states that the glory of God came from the East.

Also the Angel of Revelation 7:2 comes from the East.

Babylon, who was conquered by Cyrus, also comes from the East (Isaiah 46:11).

Cyrus, who represents Jesus and His kings, came from the East (also known as Heaven) to destroy spiritual Babylon.

You will see that in Revelation 16:12 the drying up support of Babylonian adherents and the people turning away from Babylon, prepared the way of Jesus' coming.

The plagues will make it clear that every person stands by his own choices. The problem with sin will not be settled in God's universe until it is known to everyone that Satan's charges against God are fake. Everyone on Earth must decide their own destiny by their own choices. Those lost ones would never choose to change. No matter what God has done to influence them (Isaiah 3:10, 11). The last events of Earth prove the saints would rather die than to deny faith in Jesus. They also showed that if permitted, the wicked would kill God's people based off of pure hatred and rebellion. It will be shown what life would be like if Satan were in control of the universe. At last, all beings will be totally clear in regards to God's marvelous plan for people and his justice in dealing with those who rebel against him.

At last every knee shall bow, and every tongue confess, including Satan and his angels. That God has been just and kind, and that every lost human being and angel is lost because he willfully chose a lifestyle of rebellion even after fully understanding the folly of sin and disobedience. Then, and only then, can the sinner safely be destroyed (Romans 14:11, Philippians 2:10, 11).

The entire sinful world is arranged on one side with Satan as its leader, and on other side, the Kings of the East (Jesus and his kings). Armageddon refers to the destruction or slaughter of the unsaved at Jesus' coming. The "gathering" together for the battle of Revelation 16:14, 16 refers to the unifying of religionists of all kinds, world-wide. It is not limited to a small battle area. The Battle of Armageddon, during which the wicked are destroyed, is described in Revelation 1:7, 6:14-17, 14:19-20, 16:17-21, 17:14, and 19:11-21. The wicked are about to destroy God's people when the Lord returns and the wicked are instead destroyed in what is called Armageddon. At the 1,000 years, the wicked still have the same bitter hatred of God and his people. They also still carry the same desire to destroy them. So they surround the Holy City to capture it. At that point, the final portion of Armageddon takes place as the wicked are destroyed by fire (Revelation 20:9). The warning here is unless we seek him daily and keep our relationship with him at top priority, we could end up surprised and lost in that great day. This is the message from The One who is Holy and True:

"He has the key that belongs to David, and when he opens a door, no one can close it. And when he closes it, no one can open it. Thy works behold. I have set an opened door before thee, no man can shut it: for thy has a little strength and my name has not been denied. Those who said they were Jesus and are not, I will make them of the Synagogue of Satan. I will make them come worship my feet, and know that I love thee. The word of my patience has been kept, I will keep thee from the hour of temptation upon the world which shall come, to try those who dwell upon the Earth.

5

The Origin of Satan

Did God create a Devil? What is the source of evil in the world in which we live? The Bible reveals the origin of the being who tempted our first parents, the one who continues to deceive mankind until today. Isaiah 14:12 mentioned a "great creator" named Lucifer. Lucifer, a super archangel which sat on a throne, a cherub, having been at the very throne of God in Heaven. God had placed Lucifer in the position to govern the Earth, administering over Earth's angels. Happiness, peace, joy, of Earth was Lucifer's doing. God told Lucifer, "From the moment you were created, you lived a perfect life, until you were discovered doing wrong." God did not create a devil, he created a beautiful, perfect, super-angel. Lucifer had allowed his beauty and perfection to fill him with vanity, self-glory, self-desire. He became envious of God's power and resented the power in which God had over him. He plotted with his angels and coerced them into an army that would invade the Heaven of God in order to knock God off the throne of the universe. Lucifer was going to be God. It is his deceptive sway over the "Prince of Tyre" that will cause his personage to claim that he, a man, is God. So Lucifer was no longer the "light-bringer", but now an adversary, an aggressor, a competitor, an enemy. In fact, Satan is a Hebew translation for "betrayer". One third of God's angels who had decided to follow

Lucifer's lead in the rebellion had become demons. That then lead to chaos on Earth.

It is a battle waged by spirits throughout. A battle fought before man's creation. Lucifer was not content with administering God's government on the Earth, rather, it is clear that he sought to ascend above the clouds and to invade the Kingdom of Heaven itself. He wanted to exalt his throne above every other being and to embody God himself. God cut this rebellion short. Lucifer and the angels that followed him were cast back down to Earth. Jesus told his disciples that he had seen Lucifer, now known as Satan, fall as lightning from Heaven (Luke 10:18).

The spirit being, Satan, had become completely perverted in his thinking as a result of choices that he had made. He was then, and is now, a source of lies and deceit. Satan is constantly seeking to ensnare mankind. God has continued to allow Satan to hold sway over the Earth for an important reason, until Jesus Christ returns to remove him (Revelation 20:1-3). Mankind, having chosen the way of trial and error (Genesis 3:1-6) rather than the way of divinely revealed knowledge, is being allowed to write the lesson of human experience. After giving Satan six millennial "days" in which to work, God will finally remove him and reserve the seventh 1,000 year "day" for himself. Finally, the great God will truly set his hand to save this miserable and unhappy world by sending Jesus Christ back in power and glory to set up his kingdom. In the meantime, he will have allowed human beings to experience the results of Satan's way, and then to have 1,000 years of God's way as a contrast.

Truly, God's ways are great and wondrous!

1. Was King David a man after God's own heart? (Acts 13:22)

2. Peter gave his sermon on the Day of Pentecost, 50 days after Christ's resurrection and 10 days after his ascension. At the time of this sermon, had King David ascended to Heaven or was he still in his grave awaiting the resurrection? (Acts 2:34)

3. When the Apostle John wrote his gospel, more than 60 years after Christ's resurrection, had anyone but Christ yet ascended to heaven? (John 3:13)

4. What is the reward of the true Christians as recorded in Revelation 5:10?

5. Is it appointed to all men once to die? (Hebrews 9:27)

6. Does Paul tell us in Hebrews 11:13 that Enoch, like Abel and Noah (vv. 4, 5-7) died in faith? Has he yet received the promises of God? (Hebrews 11:13, 39-40)

7. "Enoch was translated that he should not see death." Enoch walked in God's way making him worthy to escape the future Second Death, which will destroy the incorrigibly wicked. Does Revelation 20:6 speak of a second death? Will all who ultimately share in the first resurrection be "translated"? (Colossians 1:13)

8. What will happen to the wicked dead? (Revelation 20:14-15) Will they meet their final fate after the Millenium is over? (Revelation 20:4-6, 14)

9. Will the wicked burn forever or will they be burned up? (Malachi 4:1-3)

10. Was the hellfire that Jesus spoke of something capable of destroying both "body and soul"? (Matthew 10:28)

6

The Bible Describes Three Heavens and Three Hells?

The First Heaven:

This is also called the Firmament or expanse of Heaven.

It is the Heaven where the birds fly and where the clouds give rain.

- Genesis 1:26 - "The birds of the air" (Heavens)

- Genesis 2:20 - "Adam gave names to the birds of the air."

- Genesis 8:2 - "The rain from Heaven was restrained."

- 1 Kings 18:45 - "That the sky became black with clouds."

<u>The Second Heaven:</u>

- *Genesis 22:17 - "That in blessing I will Bless thee, and in multiplying I will multiply the seed as the stars of the Heaven, and as the sand which is upon the seashore; and thy seed shall possess the gate of his enemies."*

- *Exodus 32:13 - "Remember Abraham, Isaac, and Israel, thy servants, to whom thouswarest by thine own self, and said unto them, I will multiply your seed as the stars of Heaven, and all this land that I have spoken of will I give unto your seed, and they shall inherit it forever."*

- *Joshua 10:13 - "And the sun stood still, and the moon stayed, until the people had avenged themselves upon their enemies, is not written in the book of Ja'Sher? So the sun stood still in the midst of Heaven, and hasted not to go down about a whole day."*

<u>The Third Heaven:</u>

The Apostle Paul tells us that the heaven of God's abode is the "Third Heaven". This is often designated by the phrase "the Heaven of Heavens".

- Joshua 2:11 - "God in Heaven"

- Psalm 11:4 - "The Lord is in his Holy Temple, Lord is in Heaven."

- 2 Corinthians 12:2 - "I can not tell; (whether in the body, I cannot tell; or whether out of the body, I cannot tell: God knoweth;) such one caught up in the third heaven."

<u>The First Hell; Sheol or Hades:</u>

Those are the Hebrew & Greek words for "the grave".

The Bible never referred to a place of consciousness or torment, but the graves where the dead wait for resurrection.

- Genesis 37:35 - "For I will go down into the grave unto my son mourning."

- Proverbs 15:11 - "Hell and destruction are before the Lord: how much more than the hearts of the children of men?"

- Ecclesiastes 9:10 - "For there is no work, nor device, nor knowledge, nor wisdom, in the grave whither, thou goest."

- Matthew 11:23 - "And thou, Capernaum, which are exalted unto Heaven, shall be brought down to Hell."

- 1 Corinthians 15:55 - "O death, where is thy sting? O grave, where is thy victory."

<u>*The second Hell, Gehenna:*</u>

Named in the New Testament as a "place of destruction".

- *Matthew 5:22 - "I say unto you, whoever is angry with his brother without a cause shall be in danger of the Judgement and whosoever say to brother Raca, shall be in danger of the council: but whosoever shall say, thou fool, shall be in danger of hell fire."*

- *Matthew 10:28 - "And fear not them which kill the body, but are not able to kill the soul: but rather fear him which is able to destroy both soul and body in hell."*

<u>The Third Hell, Tartaroo:</u>

The place of restraint where the demon spirits placed their rebellions against God.

- *2 Peter 2:4 - "For if God spared not the Angels that sinned, but cast them down to hell, and delivered them into chains of darkness, to be reserved unto judgement."*

7

How Absolutely Vital it is For Christians to Understand and to Experience the Prayer of Paul.

The God of our Lord Jesus Christ, the Father of Glory, may give unto you a spirit of wisdom and Revelation in the knowledge of Him (Ephesians 1:17). It means life or death to our Christian life.

The Bible states, that "May any of you lack wisdom, ask God and he will generously give to all without reproach." Wisdom and revelation by the Spirit God of our Lord Jesus, Father of Glory, may give you a spirit of sound mind.

8

The Spirit of Wisdom and Revelation

When Jesus opened the scriptures to his disciples their hearts were burning within them.

9

Foundation of Wisdom and Knowledge

- *Revelation 1:17 - "And when I saw him, I fell at his feet as dead. But he laid his right hand out to me."*

Paul's purpose in writing Galatians is clear; to expose the false gospel preached by the Judaizers.

- *Revelation 3:1 - "And unto the Angel of the Church in Sardis write; These things said he that hath the Seven Spirits of God and the Seven Stars; I know thy works; that thou hast a name that thou livest, and art dead."*

10

Christ, the "Prince of Peace"

He alone has the power to really bring peace! "The increase of his government and peace will be no end." With Christ as the World Ruler, mankind will recover from the terrible devastation that preceded his coming, humans will begin multiplying and replenishing the Earth, the laws and ways of God's government will spread among the globe.

Satan get thee

behind me!

You have no idea how

God works!

This is the record of the events that Jesus Christ revealed.

God gave him the revelation to show his servants what must happen very soon. Christ made these things known to John, his servant, by sending his angels to him. For the time is near when all these things will happen.

From John to the Seven Churches, may grace and peace be yours from God, who is "who was" and who is "to come", and from the Seven Spirits in front of his throne. And also from Jesus Christ, the faithful witness, the first to be raised from death, and who is the ruler of the kings of the world.

"Look! He is coming on the clouds! Everyone will see him, including those who pierced him. All people on Earth will mourn over him. So shall it be! I am the first and the last", says the Lord God Almighty, who is, who was, and who is to come.

As I turned to see the voice that spoke with me, I saw seven golden candlesticks. And of the seven candlesticks, one was clothed with a garment down to the foot with a golden girdle. His head and hair were white as wool; as white as snow. His eyes were like flames of fire. His feet as if they burned in a furnace. And he had in his right hand seven stars and out of his mouth was a sharp two-edged sword. When I saw him, I fell at his feet as dead. He then laid his right hand upon me saying, "Fear not, I am the First and the Last. I am he that liveth and was dead; behold. I am alive forevermore and have the keys of hell and death. Amen."

"Remember therefore from where thou art fallen, and repent, and do the first works, or else I will come unto thee quickly, for none of these things which thou shalt suffer. Behold! The devil shall cast some of you into prison, that ye may be tried, and ye shall have tribulation ten days be thou faithful unto death, and I will give thee a Crown of Life. Repent or else I will come unto thee quickly, and I will fight them with the sword of my mouth."

Notwithstanding I have a few things against thee, because that woman Jezebel who calls herself a prophetess tried to teach and seduce my servants to commit fornication. I gave her space to repent fornication, and she repent not. Behold I will cast her into a bed and those who commit adultery with her shall go into great tribulation, unless they repent of their deeds. I will kill her children with death. I will give every one of you according to your works, as many as I love, I rebuke and chasten: be zealous therefore and repent.

After this I looked, and behold, a door was opened in heaven. The first voice which I heard was of a trumpet talking with me, which said, "Come up hither, I will show thee things which must be hereafter. And immediately I was in the spirit, a throne was set in Heaven, and one sat on the throne. And roundabout the throne were four and twenty seats. Upon the seats I saw four and twenty elders sitting, clothed in white raiment. They had on their heads crowns of gold and out of the throne proceeded lightnings and thunderings and voices. There were seven lamps of fire burning before the throne, where were the Seven Spirits of God. Before the throne there was a sea of glass like unto crystal and roundabout the throne were four beasts full of eyes before and behind.

And the first beast was like a lion, the second beast like a calf, the third beast like a face of a man, and the fourth beast like a flying eagle. And when he opened the fourth seal, I heard the voice of the fourth beast say, "Come and see". I looked and beheld a pale horse. His name that sat on him was Death, and Hell followed him. Power was given unto them over the fourth part of the Earth to kill with a sword, hunger, death, and with the beast of the Earth. When he opened the first seal, I saw under the altar the souls of them that were slain for the word of God and for the testimony which they held. They cried with a loud voice saying, "How long, O Lord, holy and true, dost thou not judge and avenge our blood on them that dwell on the Earth?" I beheld when he opened the sixth seal, and lo, there was a great earthquake. The sun became black as sackcloth of hair and the moon became red as blood, and the stars of Heaven fell unto the Earth, even as a fig tree casteth her untimely figs when she is shaken of a mighty wind.

When he opened the seventh seal, there was silence in Heaven for some time. I saw the seven angels which stood before God and to them were given seven trumpets. The angel took the censor and filled it with fire from the altar and cast it into the Earth. There were voices, great thunder and lightning, an earthquake and the seven angels who had the seven trumpets prepared themselves to sound. The first angel sounded and there followed hail and fire mingled with blood which were cast upon the Earth. The once lively trees and green grass was scorched.

The second angel sounded as if a great mountain burning with fire was cast into the sea and the third part of the sea became blood. And the third part of the creatures which were in the sea that once had life, died. The third part of the ships were destroyed and the third angel sounded. There fell a great star from Heaven burning as it were a lamp. It fell upon the third part of the rivers and upon the fountains of waters; the name of said star is called Wormwood. The third part of the waters became Wormwood and many men died of the waters because they were made bitter.

The fourth angel sounded and the third part of the sun was smitten. The third part of the moon and the third part stars were darkened, so the day shone not for a third part of it, and the night likewise. I then heard an angel flying through the midst of heaven saying with a loud voice, "Woe, woe, woe" to the people of the earth. The fifth angel sounded. I saw a star fall from heaven unto the Earth, and to him was given the key of the bottomless pit. He opened the bottomless pit and there arose a smoke out of the pit as the smoke of a great furnace. The sun and the air were darkened by the smoke of the pit. What came out of the smoke were locusts upon the earth and unto them was given power as the scorpions of the earth. It was commanded to them that they should not hurt the grass of the earth. It was told to them that they should not kill, and in those days if men are to seek death or desire to die, they shall not find it and death shall flee from them. The shapes of the locusts were like horses prepared unto battle and on their heads appeared crowns of gold, and their faces looked as if they were faces of men. They had woman-like hair, the teeth of lions, and wore breastplates. They also had tails of scorpions. Their king that reigned over them which was the angel of the bottomless pit. The sixth angel sounded and I heard a voice from the four horns of the golden altar which is before God.

He said to the sixth angel which had the trumpet, "Loose the four angels which were bound in the great river Euphrates." I saw the horses in the vision and them that sat on them, having breastplates of fire and the heads of the horses were as the heads of lions, and out of their mouths issued fire and smoke and brimstone.

I then saw another mighty angel come down from Heaven clothed with a cloud. "I will give power unto my two witnesses", the angel said. "And if any man will hurt them, fire proceedeth out of their mouth and devoureth their enemies, and if any man will hurt them he must in this manner be killed." And when they shall have finished their testimony, the beast that ascendeth out of the bottomless pits shall make war against them and shall overcome them and kill them. And their dead bodies shall lie in the street of the great city which spirituality is called Sodom and Egypt, where also our Lord was crucified. And the seventh angel sounded; and there were great voices in Heaven saying "The kingdoms of this world are becoming the kingdoms of our Lord and of Christ, and he shall reign forever and ever.

There appeared a great wonder in Heaven; a woman clothed with the sun and the moon under her feet and upon her head a crown of twelve stars, and there appeared another wonder in Heaven; a great red dragon having seven heads, ten horns, and seven crowns upon his heads. There was war in Heaven. Michael and his angels fought against the dragons and the dragon fought and his angels prevailed not; neither was their place found any more in Heaven.

And the great dragon was cast out, that old serpent called the devil, Satan which deceiveth the whole world. He was cast out into the Earth and his angels were cast out with him. I heard a loud voice in Heaven that said, "Now is come salvation, and strength, and the kingdom of our God and the power of Christ". For the accuser of our brethren is cast down which accused them before our God day and night. And the Earth helped the woman; the Earth opened her mouth and swallowed up the flood which the dragon cast out of his mouth. The dragon was wrought with the woman and went to make war with the remnant of her seed, which kept the commandments of God and had the testimony of Jesus Christ. I stood upon the sand of the sea and saw a beast rise up out of the sea having seven heads and ten horns. Upon his head were ten crowns and the name of blasphemy. And the beast which I saw was like unto a leopard, his feet were as the feet of a bear, and his mouth of a lion. The dragon gave him his power, his seat, and great authority. I saw one of his heads as if it were wounded to death and his deadly wound was healed. They worshipped the dragon which gave power unto the beast, and then they worshipped the beast.

I beheld another beast coming up out of the Earth and had two horns, a lamb, and he spake as a dragon. And he exercised all the power of the first beast before him. And he doeth great wonders and deceiveth them that dwell on the earth by the means of those miracles which he had power to do in the sight of the beast.

And that no man might buy or sell, save he that had the mark or the name of the beast. For it is the number of a man and his number is six hundred threescore and six. And I looked and lo, a lamb stood on the Mount Sion and with him one hundred and four thousand people having his father's name written in their foreheads saying with a loud voice, "Fear God and give glory to him, for the hour of his judgement is come, and worship him that made heaven and earth and the sea and the fountains of waters.

And there followed another angel saying, "Babylon is fallen, that great city, because she made all nations drink of the wine of the wrath of her fornication." Another angel came out from the altar which had power over fire. The wine press was trodden without the city and blood came out of the wine press. And the wine press was trodden without the city and blood came out of the wine press. I saw another sign in Heaven, great and marvelous; seven angels having the seven last plagues. For in them is filled up the wrath of God. I saw as it were a sea of glass mingled with fire, and them that had gotten the victory over the beast and over his image. One of the four beasts gave unto the seven angels seven golden vials full of the wrath of God who liveth forever and ever. For they have shed the blood of the saints and prophets and thou has giveth them blood to drink, for they are worthy.

I saw three unclean spirits like frogs come out of the mouth of the dragon and out of the mouth of the beast, and out of the mouth of the false prophet. For they are the spirits of devils, working miracles which go forth unto the kings of the Earth and the whole world to gather them to the battle of that great day of God Almighty.

And there were voices, and thunder, and lightning, and there was a great earthquake so mighty, an earthquake so great. The city was divided into three parts, and the cities of the nations fell and great Babylon came in remembrance before God to give unto her the cup of the wine of the fierceness of his wrath. Every island fled away and the mountains were not found. There fell upon men a great hall out of Heaven, every stone about the weight of a talent. Men blasphemed God because of the plague of the hail, for the plague thereof was exceeding great. And he said unto me, "These sayings are faithful and true: and the Lord God of the Holy prophet sent his angel to shew unto his servants the things which must shortly be done." And he saith unto me, "Seal not the sayings of the prophecy of this book, for the time is at hand."

The end of all things is at hand, your choice is heaven or perdition, your eternal destiny depends on how you respond to this choice.

11

Seven Signs Announcing Christ's Return

Natural Disasters, Nuclear War, and the Heavenly Signs Herald the Second Coming!

1. Growing danger of nuclear war

2. Earthquakes and other natural disasters

3. A united union seeks global primacy

4. A powerful leader unites billions in a religious revival

5. The abomination of desolation

6. The gospel of the Kingdom of God preached to all nations

7. Heavenly signs and the Day of the Lord

Many who watch world news and study bible prophecy know that a cosmic disturbance in the Heavens will shock everyone on Earth. Some Bible includes a header above Revelation 6:12, the sixth seal, Cosmic Disturbances.

Does it mean the recent "blood moon" Lunar eclipses that captured so much attention?

"I looked when he opened the sixth seal, and behold, there was a great earthquake, and the sun became black as sackcloth of hair, the moon became like blood, and the stars of Heaven fell to the

Earth as a fig tree drops its late figs when it is shaken by a mighty wind. Then the sky receded as a scroll when it is rolled up, and every mountain and island was moved out of its place. The kings of the Earth, the great men, the rich men, the commanders, the mighty men, every slave, and every free man, hid themselves in the caves and in the rocks of the mountains and saith to the mountains and rocks, "Fall on us and hide us from the face of him who sits on the throne and from the wrath of the lamb! For the great day of his wrath has come, and who is able to stand?"

www.ingramcontent.com/pod-product-compliance
Lightning Source LLC
Chambersburg PA
CBHW070818170726
48000CB00018B/1323